God you are healing. You are amazing and you are blessing my life abundantly. Thank you for your gifts, energy, and life to us! GOD you are beyond great and nobody can stop what you do to bless us! When you are on my side, I am unstoppable and a force that cannot be dismantled! Thank you God!

You have never failed me God. I am still standing in your righteous glory making an impact on life! Thank you! You pushed me

through and you kept me going here today!

Keep faith and you will be blessed!

We can face any challenge. I am enough to face all challenges. I will never stop and I must keep going.

I won't lose and I will maintain my will to keep going. Make notice to your growth and keep growing. God you are healing, thank you! Thank you for being great to me. Through every pain and through every struggle, you have brought me out whole. I am divine in your image of likeliness. I am prospering through your grace. I am delivered through your mercy and forgiveness. I have not given up and I never will. I must strive and

I will thrive. I have confessed my wrongdoings. Therefore I am led to my progress. God you are healing! My peace and sanity are gifted within me! Thank you God! I humbly honor you Lord and give reverence to your name and to your way. Jesus is the way and is my light to conquer every day! Let's keep moving and let's keep healing! Thank you God you are healing!

God you have never failed me. You lifted me up and carried me on my way! To a brighter tomorrow and better day! You've made a way through my day. God, thank you!

Be strong and don't give up on you !

Make a way out to prosper in your name God.

Don't fear your success. Don't fear what you

can do well at! Keep going. I know it feels like

no one may not be helping you but God is

pushing you forward. Watch as you grow GOD will continue to have people guide you forward in life. God has no limits and God will have no limits with your life! **Seek God in everything you do. Put God first as always.**

God has dominion over the success in your life! Never forget about what God can make happen to your life and no need to worry of what God can do to your life!

Thankfulness for God. The love for God shines brightly over everything. You gain comfort in uncomfortable situations! You gain joy in great situations!

Write down your thoughts with God. Write down your suffering. You have been on the wheel for too long now. Let God encourage you. Make your life change with God. Your ways with God. Be enthusiastic for God!

Praise

Highly for God.   Have reverence and humble

yourself to God. AND GOD shall make room

for you. God will go high for you. God will

move obstacles away from you and carry you over. Let God take the wheel. Let God drive for you around in life! You´ve been on the wheel too long now. It's time to let GOD take over. God can deal with it better. God can

heal and love you right!

Don't hold yourself down no more.

DOnt look down on you anymore. Look up to

God when you worry, when you feel trouble around. Look, try it right now, and take a breath with God. It feels great, right! That is because God is our way. Our way and our path! God is our protection and God is showing us Godś love. Hold it tight to your heart and soul and walk firmly through your life! God I love you! The joy flows and Fulfills my spirit and in everyone to look to you!

You've made me abundant, whole and

spiritual!

I give reverence to your work in life!

Thank you for your grace and favor.

Let's keep moving, God strengthened your roots to make you stand firm against any challenge and not be easily pushed over but you can get back up and surmount them.

God you protect me! It has got me

through the fire. Carried me high in life!

Helping others fly through life! This is my year

to shine. This is the moment to win. This is my

send to prosper to succeed and be great at!

Bless be to the one who honors God and

does God's work with a righteous heart, mind

and spirit with clear and pure intentions to serve and value people! We are changing ! Changing for greater! Changing for your blessings! Changing for your love God!

Changing in your arm God. Thank you God for

the strength for the will beating my veins!

God thank you! By putting God first is the gift to my heart and life! Loving God is all to my soul. It brings me joy! Thank you God!

It's ok to rest. It's ok to give yourself the time of day! The time of need to self reflect. Thank you God for the gift of hope and to put forth actions! Thank you God for planning and relaxation!

Keep going far in your life! Never stop your flow. Go with your blessings! Appreciate the moments you receive the moments you gain out of life! Love your life! Love your life!

Do yourself a favor and love your life!

Live your life fully! Don't worry about rumors

or give yourself false delusions about your

relationships with other people. They come

and they go when you work on you and have

a strong reputation. That is God protecting

and honoring you.

Lean on God fully and the right people

will come to you! Don't not be afraid to win!

Go win! Dominate and surmount in life! Life is all possible for you! Your blessings come more when you flow with life. You are rich and abundant in your spirit. God made you for a soul purpose and designed you to dominate

your goals!

Love yourself, love your worth! Get

through and build through! Life knocks you

down sometimes and it is up to us to get back up! The get up becomes much stronger than the knock down! Life can knock you down but we can come right back up!

You develop stronger and wiser! For if the next time you may fall down! You will figure out how to climb back up and make a way with God! You have to dream big and not be scared of your greatness! The great work you can manifest! Yes it does take great

strength to make it happen and your life is

worth it.

Thank you for forgiveness! Thank you for your love and peace and will power God!

This is my burst of love, harmony and peace with God! When you truly love God, nothing will stop your flow! When you love God, you love yourself. Jam enough to dominate all challenges!

No more wasting time to complain or be jealous when this emotion leads into a negative motion. A negative flow can manifest. Become aware of this matter because it has to be overridden. It can hurt your life. Do not serve a purpose that is detrimental to your life. Boost your life by embracing the love and care you need to help strengthen your own life! Pay attention and focus on the ideas you have been accruing to

naturally build your life up.

Cycle those positive ideas to cycle in

positive moments and spiritual, financial,

emotional and mental abundance to your life

in a phenomenal way! God designed it to be

and help you in life!

For those that felt like they couldn't see

God's vision for them. Keep walking, faith

flows in the rest of your journey! You have to feel it before seeing it! The more you walk, the closer you get towards seeing God's vision for your life! Keep walking to God's light out of the darkness.God you are healing. You pour light love and positive force to our hearts.

Thank you God for your presence!

Thank you God for the healing. Thank you for allowing me to follow my dreams! God you have blessed you to balance work, school and ministry! Thank you for making me tough, whole and forgiving. Transcending my life to greater tasks and bigger obstacles to face conqueror and dominate! I love you for strengthening me. WHen people doubted me, You helped me lean and focus more on love! It's not worth it to be violent but to stand up in the name of Love in the name of which God is the most powerful in everything!

GOd we know you are amazing and We love you now! We are unstoppable and the devil can't touch us now! BLess up and peace with you forever. For God you are healing, Thank you!

Do not forget how much God has brung you through in your past! Yes it rains on us all and we simply grow from it! Thanks to God! God you are healing.

Mediate to your heart

Let it breathe in peace

Love comes to us and pushes us

I know for me There is nothing better than bringing joy to another person's spirit. I'm going full on with my life and I will not surrender. I must use my will power to break through. Yes it is hard and difficult but i would rather find out what God got for me. I will be willing to go through the cuts and bruises for my God and bear the cross!!!

Luke 14:27- And whoever does not carry their cross and follow me cannot be my disciple.

Carry your weight and struggle with God and God will know you are ready to receive more blessings and can manage them and not be scared of them. Keep pushing forward and fighting for your dreams!

Do what you have to and win in the loft!

Make that shift!

Elevation,

One step to the next

God reaches us in our hearts.

I can clearly visualize God's light protecting in and near me with the angels guiding me through and helping me stay uplifted! This is a lovely experience we should not be afraid of.

If we are less of it will happen in our lives.

God puts more into your life when you are

ready to handle things righteously and

accordingly.

I live for God.

I love God.

I need God.

God is great.

Merciful GOD thank you for this day

IN Jesus name father God, you are great.

GOD you are healing.

I thank my future self in advance and I thank

my past for the experience well learned from.

I am free

No resent

No blame

No anger for what happened.

My peace is blessed from God now.

I ask God to remove toxic situations out of my

life to establish more peace.

People who I thought were my friends;

eventually left out in my life.

Ask and God will deliver the more you move

with God.

God rebukes all weapons formed against you.

None of them will prosper.

God will only incline you up mountains to

success in your life!

My God is an awesome God.

Powerful and Loving.

Constant movement with grace to help and honor God's children.

Keep moving no matter what.

Because No matter what, God got this in control for you.

You have to fully submit to God for God to fully bless you.

See you may be blocking your blessings because you may be scared of receiving the power it maintains.

Walk in the courage and that bright power

that God has blessed you with. Why because

it is made for you to use it.

And God is such a fair and living God.

God will just break you into your powerful self

to move strongly and encourage people.

When God has a plan for you, that plan will be

made through!

God brings the angels to force things to work

on your favor and on your behalf.

Keep working well.

Stay focused on your goals.

Spend time on yourself.

I am able to Progress because I enjoy

spending time with myself again. I enjoy

building things on my own. I can get this done

on my own with God. God told me to spend

more time with myself and I shall push your

life better and faster than it ever was before.

This is to help grow your life!

Even for my book, I do my best to not look

and see how much I have got done so far.

Keep moving, do not be complacent and do not be too comfortable.

God keep giving me strength

Keep giving me power and energy to keep going!

Be wise, God can work anything.

Be wise to learn from other people's mistakes

and not repeat the same mistake.

It's up to you to learn or not

Repeat the same let down someone else did. Especially when you know you can do better and not repeat a thing that can be avoided and not slow down your progress or limit it. This your decision at the end of the

day

It is really up to you on what you do.

Freedom of choice is your right.

Believe in yourself

I am the poet of courage

I am the writer of joy

I am a believer in gratitude

The joy of the Lord is my strength, I will not

fear

Respect and Love God and you can respect

and love people with ease.

You allow God to flow through you and your

work to perform righteously.

Everything is timely

Now is the right time to do the right thing.

Focusing on the present now.

You are needed now.

You are guided now.

You are Connected to the source of God now.

You are connected to God now

That is where enlightenment starts.

It is the foundation of everything including

self.

It is the foundation of finding self into your

true self.

In you, it starts from the bottom-up.

When you Build a great spirit and you

automatically build a great mind.

You know what it is like coming from the

bottom and making it to the top.

A great spirit is also a humble spirit because it

already has that security within to understand

that it is great. A great spirit doesn't have to brag and be arrogant about it.

On the contrary to The high minded person, yet low spirit; that person would think they are superior to all and have zero humility or supply much gratitude for things giving them help. They only see themselves as a great person to always be talked about or bowed down too. They may see themselves as an untouchable being and never feel the need to have empathy for what it's like to be

grounded or being an underdog or

overcomer. They would typically pick on

people feeling like an outcast. They may

believe to never struggle or feel like they have no weaknesses.

A High and loving spirit is the opposite :) . A high, loving and energetic Spirit knows what it is like to be down because with a high spirit you are grounded and you are from the core.

They give energy to rejuvenate and not

disintegrate a good heart of a person. You are

the foundation and the beginning for which

you are stood on and built for.

WIth high spirit you deeply care about everyone's feelings and you are sincere about what you mean and say to people. You are realistically sensitive to people's thoughts and your own to give.

You act in to give because you know how it is

to feel alone and on your own.

Because it is your duty to give light and

liberate others.

You act in power because you know what the journey has been like building towards. Love you understand the finding because you took the time to put it and express it from yourself to keep moving forward in life.

You change because it is right to change and

transform.

In order to do so in growth, you must change,

transform and become.

Thank you God, You are great, you are healing. And yes God can get you through it. The vision is within us all. You can do it for anyone's life, and with that we give thanks. God you are healing!

Trust God and have your spirit renewed and refreshed.

AS you believe in God, you gain more belief in yourself.

You realize nothing can stop you but you.

The GOD in you is only empowering and we must take hold and lead in that with God. Keep your energy focused and move onto God.

You are the power and change and decision make to your life.

Your influence has a major impact on the way you style up your life.

Maintain your focus, know what you want and put your vision from God into place and go implement what you see in your mind. Know God is really always there and will never forsake you.

God, you are a massive presence of love,

positivity and great will!

Take ownership of your gift, feel pride in it!

Go move in your power strongly.

Move fearlessly, and be fierce in it

Dominate in your craft.

The gift you have been blessed with.

The God I serve is the greatest!

In God's image and likeness I am great too.

Bring your success high.

Keep making your dreams happen.

You were made to!

Keep dominating in life .

You got one life at this!

You can make the best out of it.

Keep your focus high, labor high and push higher in life.

Your success and future awaits you.

You have in you too build and establish a great life.

Life is everything we make it to be.

You believe in the wisdom you can gain.

Trust yourself to make good decisions.

God is there to guide your intuition.

There is joy in listening to your heart.

Even when something doesn't turn out like you wanted it too.

God has ways to protect and strengthen your spirit, even if your heart gets pain.

Pain may be in the night but joy comes in the morning!

Thank you, God you are healing!

Look high, keep a positive vibration to your life and have clarity to your vision.

Do what you love!

Faith keeps going strongly.

Love flows greatly.

It flows in you.

And you can express it out of you.

To help someone

Liberate their spirit and free their mind with

beautiful and inspiring thoughts.

Do you believe in you?

The vision God gave you.

We are moving and growing.

Hold and express your gifts.

Space is being made in your life!

Walk with me God!

I know you are here with me!

Thank you for your presence

Thank you God in Jesus Name!

Son of God, who heals the sick and helpless!

God You Are Healing !

Dedication

This is dedicated to all my friends and family and everyone who needs that extra joy and motivation to value and keep perspective on what to have gratitude in and what you can do and not focus on what you can not do. God has given you a story to not only go through, but to show and tell! Your story may have pain in it, but you can flip that pain into power and connectivity to other people who can resonate and who may be going through what I have been through; this is to those who have been feeling like their struggle is too much to gain insight and overcome from. God has made you strong and it is going to take your strength and willpower and fire in your spirit

and heart to push you right through

everything in front of you.

Copyrights 2020 © By Jaron Mcneil

All rights and content are reserved to the sole owner of this book. This book may not be resold or reproduced in any manner.

ISBN: 978-1-71605-309-2

ABOUT ME

Hi everyone, my name is Jaron Mcneil. I love inspiring people. The greatest things I believe to connect and give to people is love, joy and encouragement. There is always a moment I seek to help someone. No feeling, thing or emotion is greater than that! I am 20 years old now and I am an empowerment speaker, Author and writer of two books now! Videos out on social media everyday. Glory to God, and my website is out right now. I am only doing my best to follow GOD's will! I am going to be a part of the change to the world and my dreams are coming into reality! Thank you

God for now and everything in advance! Be grateful and focus on what you can do and not focus on what you can't do.

My Website: Officialjaronmcneil.com

My Social Media Handles:

Instagram- Jaronisphenomenal

Twitter: Jaron A. Mcneil

Facebook: Jaron Mcneil

Youtube: Jaron_

Linkedin: Jaron Mcneil

Acknowledgements

Thank you to my family and friends for

helping me build my inspiration up and help

me also to keep to the positive and be me!

Shout to you and all that you do. I love you

and I love everyone who supports what I do

and is currently reading this message! I wish

you a blessed and amazing day!

www.ingramcontent.com/pod-product-compliance
Lightning Source LLC
Chambersburg PA
CBHW071731090426
42738CB00011B/2459